★ ALL-TIME ★
BEST ATHLETES

FOOTBALL SUPERSTARS

PERCY LEED

LERNER PUBLICATIONS ◆ MINNEAPOLIS

Lerner Publications Company
An imprint of Lerner Publishing Group, Inc.
241 First Avenue North
Minneapolis, MN 55401 USA

For reading levels and more information, look up this title at www.lernerbooks.com.

Main body text set in Mikado.
Typeface provided by HVD Fonts.

Image credits: Vic Stein/Getty Images, p. 5; David Madison/Getty Images, p. 6; George Gojkovich/Getty Images, pp. 9, 12; Bruce Bennett/Getty Images, p. 10; Focus On Sport/Getty Images, pp. 14, 17; John Biever/Icon Sportswire/Getty Images, p. 18; John Biever/Getty Images, p. 21; Cliff Welch/Icon Sportswire/Getty Images, p. 23.
Design element: FoxGrafy/Shutterstock; Anna Golant/Shutterstock.
Cover: AP Photo/Greg Trott.

Designer: Kim Morales
Lerner team: Martha Kranes

Library of Congress Cataloging-in-Publication Data

Names: Leed, Percy, 1968- author.
Title: Football superstars / Percy Leed.
Description: Minneapolis : Lerner Publications, [2024] | Series: Lerner sports rookie. All-time best athletes | Includes bibliographical references and index. | Audience: Ages 5–8 years | Audience: Grades K–1 | Summary: "Football is full of great players. But only some players have made football history. Explore the stats and careers of the best of the best in football"— Provided by publisher.
Identifiers: LCCN 2023039259 (print) | LCCN 2023039260 (ebook) | ISBN 9798765625729 (lib. bdg.) | ISBN 9798765628188 (pbk.) | ISBN 9798765632369 (epub)
Subjects: LCSH: Football—Juvenile literature. | Football players—Rating of—Juvenile literature.
Classification: LCC GV950.7 .L443 2024 (print) | LCC GV950.7 (ebook) | DDC 796.332092/2—dc23/eng/20231023

LC record available at https://lccn.loc.gov/2023039259
LC ebook record available at https://lccn.loc.gov/2023039260

Manufactured in the United States of America
1-1010184-51906-12/22/2023

TABLE OF CONTENTS

Turn the pages to meet the best football players. Count them down from 10 to 1. Number 1 is the best NFL player ever!

MEET THE 10 BEST FOOTBALL PLAYERS!

10. OTTO GRAHAM

Otto Graham won game after game. He played quarterback for the Cleveland Browns.

COUNT IT!

NFL championships: 3

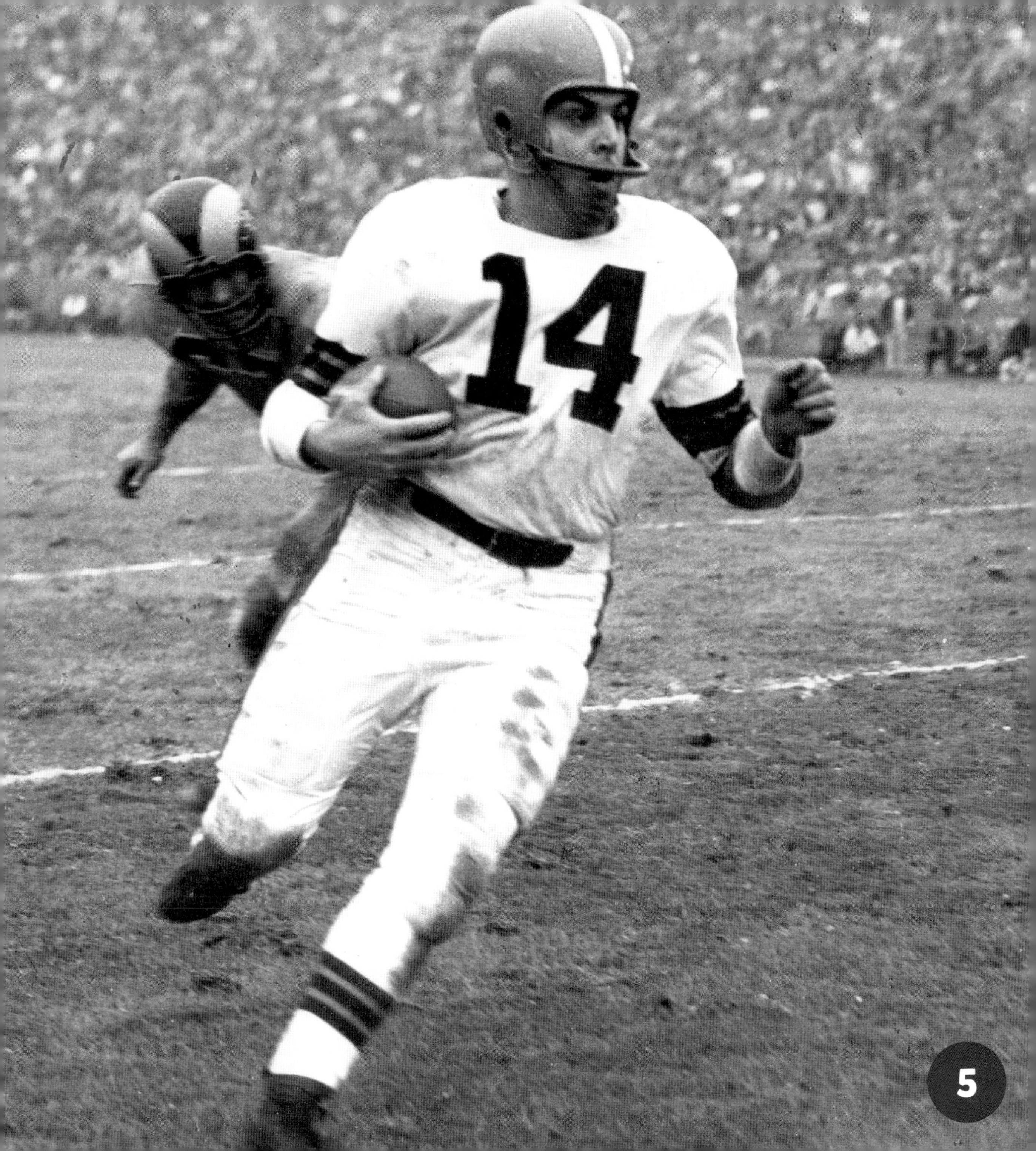
14

9. JOE MONTANA

Joe Montana always kept his cool. The quarterback played his best in the biggest games.

COUNT IT!

Super Bowl wins: 4

8. ANTHONY MUÑOZ

Anthony Muñoz was quick and strong. He blocked defenders to protect his quarterback.

COUNT IT!

Pro Bowls: 11

78

7. DON HUTSON

Don Hutson was a great wide receiver. He made up new plays that players still use.

COUNT IT!

NFL championships: 3

6. BARRY SANDERS

Barry Sanders ran with speed and power. He could spin around defenders trying to tackle him.

COUNT IT!

Rushing yards: 15,269

Riddell

32
32

5. JIM BROWN

Jim Brown was a big and strong running back. He could run over defenders.

4. LAWRENCE TAYLOR

Lawrence Taylor was a tough defender. His size and strength made him hard to stop.

3. REGGIE WHITE

Reggie White was a strong defender. Other teams needed two players to block him.

COUNT IT!

Sacks: 198

2. JERRY RICE

Jerry Rice was always ready to win. The wide receiver played for 20 NFL seasons.

COUNT IT!

Super Bowl wins: 3

80

1. TOM BRADY

Quarterback Tom Brady played for over 20 seasons. He went to the Super Bowl 10 times.

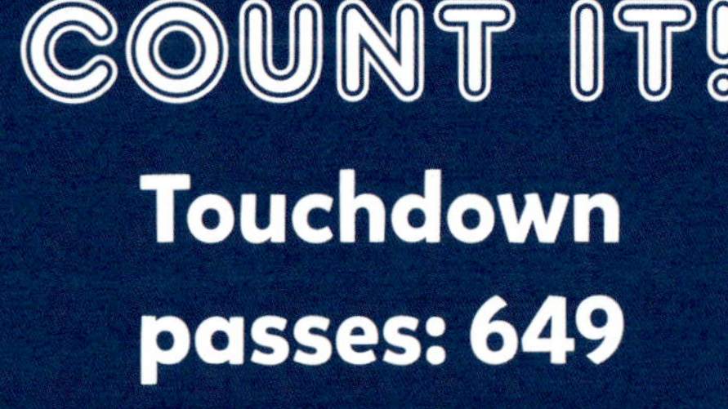

NOW IT'S YOUR TURN.

Who do you think are the best football players of all time? Make your own list!

GLOSSARY

NFL: short for National Football League

Pro Bowl: the NFL's all-star game

sack: to tackle the quarterback for a loss of yards

wide receiver: a football player whose main job is to catch passes

LEARN MORE

Adamson, Heather, and Thomas K. Adamson. *Curious about Flag Football*. Mankato, MN: Amicus, 2024.

Flynn, Brendan. *Football*. Minneapolis: A & D Xtreme, 2023.

Leed, Percy. *Football: A First Look*. Minneapolis: Lerner Publications, 2023.

INDEX